How to Raise a Teenager

Navigating the Crazy and Confusing Adolescent Years As a Parent.

By Lita Caine

Table of Contents

How to Raise a Teenager

Teenagers are not a fan of their parents. That's what most people assume. However, if you communicate with your child and listen to them without passing any judgment, you can raise a responsible teenager. All teenagers want is freedom and independence, which presents you with the perfect opportunity to teach them responsibility and show them what life has in store for them.

From bridging the gap between teenagers and parents through communication to disciplining them using teachable moments and setting consequences, and resolving conflicts, this eBook will teach you how to do it all and more. If your teenager doesn't respect you, then it's probably because you are setting high standards for them and not following them yourself. By giving them the freedom to say yes, no or by giving them time to think on the matter, you allow them to tap into their values and make a decision they feel is right and good for them. If they stumble and fall, don't give them your hand to get up but use your words to encourage them to get back up on their feet.

Introduction

Parenting teens is an art, with a bit of luck thrown in. Yes, the job can be stressful and frustrating at times, but it can be exciting, fulfilling, and fun once you figure out the secret.

Just keep in mind that none of your parenting methods should aim at *controlling* your teenager, or you will lose them.

It might feel like you don't influence your child in the years from 5 to 12, but they do pick up on your habits while growing. When it comes to teens, their behavior is correlated to the strength of your bond with them.

Usually, a good relationship between parents and teenagers is formed by success at school and general happiness. In contrast, a conflictual or weak relationship is formed when teenagers start experimenting with alcohol and drugs, hang out with the wrong crowd or perpetrate a crime.

So, how does a parent help this person blossom into a confident and strong adult?

Be Their Friend and a Parent

Teenagers crave security in the form of their parent's approval. This approval is not on good grades or doing their chores but on understanding what the teenager is going through.

For example, if a teenager takes out the car without the parent's permission and they later find out what happened, instead of acting first and talking later, they should find out the motive behind their behavior. It could be that the teenager wanted to go to a party and they knew their parents would insist on driving them, so they took the car. They wanted to avoid the embarrassment of having a helicopter parent. This might be hurtful to you. However, if you look at the situation from your teenager's perspective, you will understand where they are coming from.

This doesn't mean that such an action should go unpunished. Here's a great way to handle this situation:

"I know you think that you can't come to me with such problems, but that's not true. I would have dropped you a block away from the party."

It's a simple statement but will have a huge impact on your kid. They will look at you differently because you didn't dismiss their problem as childish.

Now comes the punishment part. You need to make them understand that they made a mistake, so they know why they are being punished.

"You know what you did was not right, and that's why you need to accept your punishment graciously."

Along with a friendly relationship, teenagers also seek independence. At times you might feel they are shutting you out, but that's not the case. Giving your teenager some responsibility, which they can easily manage, can be a great way to show them how much you trust them.

You need to navigate the closeness in a way that feels acceptable to your teenager. This way, they will be able to see that you are not trying to control them. As a result, they will share more with you.

Just remember: Always give your teenager importance over anyone else. You have to be there for them physically and emotionally. Your teenager is more likely to respect you if you extend them the same courtesy.

We understand that you want to be close to your teenager, but in some cases, you will have to say 'No.' However, don't do it often, or your teenager might feel that you are restricting them.

Boundaries must always be set in a way so that both you and your teenager respect them. At times, you will find your teenager looking towards you for advice and direction. That's when you will have to show them how you can be their parent and a friend. It will be a win-win situation when your teenager will not only listen to you but also act on your advice in a way that makes both you and them happy.

In our previous eBook, "How to Raise a Child," we talked about how to come to terms with the decision of becoming a parent. We touched on topics such as keeping your child happy, teaching them problem-solving skills, and helping them deal with their emotions.

This last eBook in the series will cover the final chapter of raising a teenager into adulthood. We will discuss what kind of personality your teenager has, how to set boundaries, how to give responsibility, and many other things that will make you give yourself a pat on the back with an "I did well."

Types of Teen Personalities

The teenage years are a doozy. Half the time, parents can't figure out what's happening. Parents have trouble understanding their teenagers because they don't know what type of personality they have.

The teen years are the most challenging because you are dealing with complex qualities that need to be carefully managed.

You are probably wondering how there can be different types of teens, right. Well, we are talking about the personality of teenagers that make them who they are.

Yes, every teenager is different, but when you combine certain character traits, you come up with multiple types. These categories give you an idea about how to handle your teenager.

Think about adults, for instance. A *worry-wart* is a person who always assumes the worst. No matter what they are talking about, the conversation takes a negative turn.

Then there's the *collector*, a die-hard fan of certain items. They never throw anything away because they think it's useful.

You wouldn't want to meet a battalion commander who organizes everything as if they are about to attack and does everything at a specified time.

Here are the most common teen types that will help you understand what kind of teenager you are living with:

When talking about a teenager, how do you picture them?

Moody, always angry at the world, thinks parents try to suppress them, etc.

The "Roller Coaster" teen is known for their mood swings. It feels like you are walking on eggshells around them. This type of teenager has one best friend, and that's their mood. They will always try to drag other people too into their orbit.

In plain and simple words: Your teenager is a big, old grump. With this teenager under their roof, parents can't seem to figure out what their mood will be when they wake up. It can go either way: good or bad.

If you have such a grumpy teenager, the first stand you need to take is to not tolerate their negativity. As a parent, you might feel compelled to fix whatever has gotten them down, but the best thing you can do for them is let them figure their own way out.

However, do look out for signs of depression. One of the most common reasons behind a rollercoaster teen's thinking is fear of judgment. This can take a dark turn and can have dangerous consequences. So, if you see them find themselves struggling with something or that they are bothered by something, step in and listen before offering your advice.

Casual Approach Teen

Does your teenager respond to everything with a shrug? Their casual approach to life matters is a cry for help. Sometimes, even in the face of a challenge, they take things easily. They don't put in the effort and assume things will resolve themselves. However, your teenager's easy-going attitude is what makes them get along with everybody, which is a point in their favor.

Their lack of motivation will make you feel down too, so when you are dealing with this type of teenager, you need to be a parent instead of a friend.

These teenagers need firm boundaries with a little push in the right direction. Make sure that they complete their chores and school work. Introduce them to responsibilities, so they can start developing independence. You don't want a Howard Wolowitz on your hands!

Fire CrackerTeen

If you have an angry one, you've got a firecracker teenager on your hands. They are the types who blow up at everything and anything. Sometimes, even when not provoked.

One of the most worrying things about a firecracker teen is that they can't take a joke. They get offended easily and usually get into a fight instead of resolving the matter through communication.

When it comes to parenting such a teenager, you need to be careful because your advice can be taken positively and negatively.

For example, you know your teenager is studying for the upcoming exam, but he can't seem to understand some of the concepts, even though they were explained in the classroom. You enter his room and see him listening to music while looking at his book. You knock on the door to get his attention so that you can ask him if he needs anything. He tells you to get a snack for him and close the door behind you, so he doesn't get disturbed. Before you close the door, you casually say, *"You know, you will understand what you are reading better without the music in your head."*

This sets him off, but he doesn't say anything. He angrily gets up and slams the door in your face.

If you are a parent to this teenager, you need to set clear rules with firm consequences so that they know their bad behavior will not be tolerated. You need to tell them that they will be punished if they misbehave.

Sometimes, the out-of-character behavior can be because of drugs. So, make sure that your teenager is not taking anyone else's prescription pills or smoking behind your back.

Fusspot Teen

As the name says, a fusspot teen is a drama queen. They are hard to please because nothing satisfies them. Still, they expect other people to do things for them and then find fault in it.

This behavior is mostly seen between siblings. For example, your older kid might boss around your younger kid and force them to do things like make their bed, fold their clothes, clean their room, etc.

If you are too soft on a fusspot teen, they might try to make you their slave. This might sound a bit over the top, but before you know it, you will be picking up their dirty dishes, making their favorite food, and giving them leeway when it comes to chores. Before you know it, your kitchen will be a 5-star restaurant, and you will be catering to your fussy teen day and night.

So, what can a parent do? In this case, setting firm limits is the only way to stop their demanding and bossy behavior. You need to tell them what's acceptable and what's not. That's it! This way, they will have to restrain their needs and find out what is their parent's responsibility and what is theirs.

Lion Tamer Teen

If your teenager is a risk-taker, you have got a problem on your hands. They will always try to test the boundaries, which can get them in trouble. You can expect them to run at any moment, at the sign of responsibility.

They will lie to you to get out of a bind, which is why you can't trust them. For example, you are washing the dishes, and it's your teenager's turn to dry them and put them on the rack. When you call her name, she says that she is studying for a test and doesn't want any distractions. You know for a fact that there's no test tomorrow because you are on a school committee.

The world needs adults with risk-taker personalities, not teenagers! They could be our future entrepreneurs because nothing holds them back.

Setting limits and agreeing on punishments are the best ways to tame these teenagers. Let the consequences teach them the error of their ways. Avoid rescuing or shielding them because they need to be knocked down to get back up.

These words might sound harsh to you, but our intention is different. Your punishment should be a teaching moment. You shouldn't shout first and talk later.

Changing a teenager's behavior can be difficult, especially when a lion tamer lives under your roof. However, you can look for safer ways to mold their risk-taking behavior with activities like rock climbing, gymnastics, and mounting biking. It's probably all the aggression in them that's causing them to act this way. A healthy outlet will allow them to get a hold of their emotions and steer their life in the right direction.

Stuck-in-the-Mud Teen

If you have a headstrong teenager, you might need to pace yourself and develop the patience to deal with them. These teenagers usually develop an obsession, which can be either good or bad.

One of the biggest characteristics of these teenagers is that they can't cope with change, which often causes discomfort to the entire family. For example, you are moving to a new city because you got transferred. Bringing your younger child on board took some convincing, but they didn't object much since they are just five years old. On the other hand, your teenager just started making friends and has something good going on here, which is why they don't want to move. The move is too overwhelming for them, and they want you to leave them behind.

If you find yourself stuck in such a situation, the best way to deal with them is through logical reasoning because they are already feeling emotional.

One of the good things about these teenagers is that they are the family's ritual keepers. For every occasion, they make sure that things go the same way as they did the first time.

You need to be gentle with a stuck-in-the-mud teenager because a big event can trip them up. So, make sure to talk about any change in advance so they can prepare for it. When you see them taking a risk that you know can do them actual harm, point out another way. They will balk at your interference, which is why you need to be a friend rather than a parent. Your advice should be unbiased and full of encouragement.

You probably wonder how teenagers, known for having hundreds of mood swings, can be divided into six categories. The teenager types mentioned above are the most common ones, and yours is bound to have a mix of some of the personalities.

The Parenting Dilemma

Parents often find themselves between a rock and a hard place. It can be extremely difficult to deal with teenagers in situations where they believe that they are right and you are wrong.

Here, the parenting dilemma enters the picture. The toughest phase in raising a child is when they turn thirteen. From hormonal changes to behavioral ones, you deal with different scenarios. As they grow up, you meet with the *rebellious* teenager, who thinks the world is out to get them.

It becomes difficult for parents to control their daily tantrums and outbursts with such thinking. As a result, they find themselves in constant worry over whether or not they are good parents.

Let's take a look at two different scenarios of parenting:

Scenario #1

Your child is eight years old, and it's his birthday. You plan on hosting a party and inviting a couple of children your son is friends with. Social etiquette dictates that you invite the entire class because your son will be talking about his birthday party at school. A hurt mom calls you saying that her daughter was crying because she didn't get an invite.

How would you handle such a situation?

Since your child is too young to comprehend the matter, you tell the hurt mom that it was a small event and you didn't call most of the children from your son's class.

Your teenager wants to host a sleepover. After much thinking, you say yes. You ask her how many people she is inviting, and she says 10. You tell her no because that's too many girls.

She shouts at you and says you are stopping her from having a good time and that you always do this. Angry, you shout back, and it all blows out of proportion. When you don't budge, she sneaks out at night and goes to her friend's house, who is going to a party with boys in it.

The point of telling you these stories is that a teenager is not a 5-year-old. They won't just sit quietly and accept your decision. They will question, act out and refrain from doing anything outright when their needs are not met, no matter how unreasonable they are.

Therefore, you need to use respectful parenting methods. Hitting your children is a big NO. Do not threaten them, intimidate them or yell at them.

Always be a gentle parent. Don't confuse this with the misconception that is permissive parenting. The former parenting method assumes that there are few or no boundaries. In gentle and respectful parenting, there are well-held and firm boundaries.

It might come off as condescending, but gentle parenting treats your teenager as a person. Often, parents assume they know what is right for their child, which is why they try to control them.

What you are forgetting is that teenagers have feelings just like parents. They have wants, needs, desires, and hopes.

However, since they have yet to learn the realities of the world, they don't know what is good for them.

This parenting method teaches you that we all make mistakes. We need to be corrected from time to time. However, since we are *parent*s, we assume all the responsibilities. Yes, teenagers are allergic to responsibilities, but it is the only way to show them the right way; this is the parenting dilemma that we all face.

The Teenage Difference

Do you find it hard to make your teenager listen to you? What about trust? What are your thoughts on it? You probably don't have any dice there either.

You might be forgetting that teenagers operate on their hormones and emotions; this makes them incredibly ruthless judges.

Has this ever happened to you: It's the weekend, and you want to spend time with your teenage son. You go up to his room and see the first barrier: The "Knock at Your Own Risk" sign. It seems harmless enough, so you knock and enter your son's room. He has his headphones on and is looking at a comic book. You face the second barrier when your son does take his headphones off. After a while, he removes them and says one word, "What?"

The one word rattles you, but you take a deep breath to calm yourself down.

"I was wondering if you would like to go out with me to the gaming arena?"

Your son looks at you and says, "Sorry, dad, I already told my friends that I would go out with them. We have one hell of a night planned, and oh, I will be sleeping at Jeremy's."

"Why don't we make it a dad and son day today? You can always go out with your friends next weekend."

"No offense dad, but I would rather hang out with my friends in a gaming zone than my dad, who doesn't even know the latest games."

Feeling disappointed, you leave the room.

Though your teenager's response was hurtful, you, too, are at fault here. One of the biggest mistakes parents make is that they don't take an interest in the current cultural points and trends their teenagers are following.

When it comes to bridging the gap between parent and teenager, you need to have some influence. You can't talk about World War II with your teenager when he is interested in football.

In the ages between 3 and 10, parents hold the status of gods. Your children look up to you, try to imitate you, and want to spend every waking moment with you. As soon as their age gets a *teen* in it, your thirteen-year-old son or daughter doesn't want your interference in their life.

Small children obey you because they think what you say is important. On the other hand, teenagers know their surroundings and believe they know what's best for them.

Find Your Connection

When your child was young, how did you connect with them?

Here are a couple of choices:

- Cuddles
- Bedtime while reading stories
- Feeding
- Bathing
- Taking them out for ice cream

This bonding time made them feel safe and secure with you. As your children grow up, their needs will change, and you'll have to look for different ways to connect with them. The task now seemed difficult because nothing held your teenager's attention for long.

Your child, who used to whine and tell you about the fight they had with their best friend and wanted snuggles to feel good, is now more interested in playing video games and hanging out with their friends.

To gain your teenager's trust, you need to show interest in what they like. That's the only way to get into their inner circle and make the relationship secure. If that means listening to how they made a dystopian world in Minecraft, so be it. If they are watching a new TV show that is too childish for your taste, make an effort to talk about it.

Remember: Spend time with your teenager but not to a degree where they start rolling their eyes at you. For example, your teenager will happily participate in a 2-hour discussion about the Avengers. However, when these 2 hours are used to explain acceptable behavior and etiquette, the conversation takes a turn for the first.

Do you know how they say that children have a short attention span? Well, teenagers have selective hearing. They will listen to what feels right to them and let the rest slip out the other ear.

So, when explaining to them something important, talk about it for 20 minutes max.

Disciplining Your Older Child

To most parents, discipline comes naturally. For example, if a child is playing a game and it's not safe, you stop them from playing it anymore.

If their friends come over, they cannot close the door, or their video games will be taken away.

If they eat all their snacks in one go, they won't get any more later in the day. It seems easy to discipline young children, but the process can be a little difficult when it comes to teens. When your child grows old and enters the teen years, they no longer see you as the god you were once to them. They have their own life, and their hopes and dreams don't revolve around you.

Here, your previous teachings and upbringing come in. For example, if you taught them the importance of saving, then by now, they will know the responsibility of spending carefully.

Disciplining at this stage does not involve reprimanding them or setting new rules. It's more about reinforcing the old ones and reminding them of the consequences they will face if they break a rule. You need to keep in mind that teenagers are the king of deflection. Sometimes they might listen to you and other times not. This is why transitioning into a friend, guide, and teacher from a parent is important. It gives you a little edge and allows you to know what your teenager is going through.

The world has changed, and the problems you face as a parent are not even close to what's bothering your teenager. They have a roof over their head, good food to eat, they get an allowance to buy whatever they want, and more luxuries that you could only dream of. Hence, you need to be one with them when building a bond with them.

Positive Parenting – A Game Plan for Raising a Teenager

As children learn new lessons and life rules during teen years, so do parents. They need to adopt new parenting techniques because they no longer deal with a 5-year-old who can be bribed with candy. As children grow and become teenagers, they start spending time away from their parents. They see them as authority figures and a buzzkill. No wonder you are having a hard time bonding with your teen!

This doesn't mean that you can give them leeway to do whatever they want. Parenting with approval and love, taking a firm yet positive approach, and not getting frustrated in situations where things don't go your way are just some of the keys to not losing your cool when dealing with a teenager. There are plenty more keys that are still being discovered to this day. So, you might have to alter your approach based on your teenager's response.

To guide your teenager, you need to adopt positive parenting strategies, such as promoting self-esteem, resolving conflict, communicating, and teaching responsibility. Let's take a look at these strategies one by one:

Positive Parenting Strategies

Promoting Self-Esteem

Having a positive image of yourself makes you feel worth loving and valuable. This applies to not just teenagers but adults and parents too.

Since teenagers spend more time with their friends, their self-image is built through the eyes of their peers and their social standing. Hence, if one of their friends jokingly says, "You are dumb," your teenager will scoff at it at the moment but think about it later.

Hence, you should regularly praise your teenager for jobs well done. It will help them build positive self-esteem. The way teens see themselves directly affects their behavior.

To foster a good image in them, here are a few suggestions:

Pay Close Attention to What Your Teenager Is Doing But Respect Their Privacy

Being involved in your teen's life shows them that you care, but you need to set a boundary for yourself. Know what extracurricular activities and courses they are taking, who their friends are, the fights they've gotten themselves in, etc.

Moreover, make an effort to the names of their friends and ask your teenager if they would like to come over.

Your involvement in your teenager's life should be to this extent only. Do not try to control them by asking what they are doing, why they are doing it, who they are hanging with, etc.

If you go online and search for positive parenting blogs, you will find the writers recommending the use of a spyware app to keep tabs on your teenager. This is a huge invasion of privacy, and if your teenager finds out, you will lose their trust.

So, don't pray for details. Wait for them to come to you.

Compliment Your Teenager and Make Sure They Know the Praise is Coming from Your Heart

Your praise matters a lot to your teenager, even if they don't show it. They will shrug off the compliment, but underneath, they glow with pride. So, whether they got an A+ or B- in their test, make sure to let them know you are proud of them. Try not to give underhanded compliments such as, "I know you can do better" or "Let's strive for an A next time."

Attend School Events

Teenagers notice when you are absent from the most important moment of their life. From ballet recitals to art shows, theater and sports, try to attend most events.

You might not be available sometimes due to an emergency, and your teenager would understand. However, that doesn't mean you use the same excuse every time.

Respect the Concerns Your Teenager Has

There's a science fair in your teenager's school, and they have chosen to build a project solo. They are afraid that those kids in the group might make something way better and cooler than him. That's definitely a possibility, and you should calm your teenager down with words of encouragement such as, "It doesn't matter. You made the project all by yourself, and that's an achievement in itself."

Remember that you should never give your teenager false hope or lift his spirits with colorful words. Stay in the real world but also let your teenager know that you stand by their side.

Don't Criticize Your Child

Criticism halts the growth of a teenager. According to a study by neuroscientists from leading US universities, the bond between a parent and a teenager takes a hit when tested by criticism. They discovered that area of the brain involved with taking the perspective of other people and emotional regulation shuts when they are criticized.

Fascinating, isn't it? So, all this time when you criticized your teenager, not only did you beat them emotionally but psychologically too.

If you don't like your teenager's behavior, instead of beating around the bush, tell them you dislike what they are doing. Whenever commenting on your teenager's activities, music, and fashion, be positive.

Help Them Gain Confidence

Your teenager is not a social butterfly, and that's alright. Many teenagers go through this phase. You need to step in and give your teenager the green light to explore what they like. When they succeed in their activity, be right there to cheer them on, and this will build up their confidence.

Those who succeed in any area of their life get the confidence to take more risks.

Don't Tease Your Child

Many teenagers are sensitive, and they get hurt easily. You need to make sure that your teasing is not hurting your teenager. They might laugh at the moment, but they will hold what you said in their heart. This can change the way they look at the world and become a bit cynical.

Communicating Effectively

Teenagers communicate with their parents, but they don't want to do it all the time. They have a concept of privacy, and they might not be comfortable with telling you everything until they have figured out the matter themselves.

This doesn't mean they are hiding something from you; rather, they want to feel independent. All you have to do is create opportunities to have a meaningful conversation with them.

Teenagers often have a complaint that their parents don't listen to them. So, you need to practice active listening. You need to pick a place and time and dedicate yourself entirely to the task at hand: Having a meaningful conversation.

When you teenager speaks, listen. When your teenager does something, pay them a compliment. Here's an example to help you understand how your conversation should go:

Your teenager is upset because they were working on a project and got stuck at a point. They have been struggling for two days in a row and haven't found a solution yet.

You notice their upset state and say, "If I am not wrong, you don't know how to fix the problem you have been having with your science project, right."

Try to understand their perspective.

"I get you are angry."

Now that they know you have been paying attention, you can avoid misunderstandings. Remember: You are not to provide a solution but listen to them and brainstorm to come up with one on their own. At the end of the conversation, always ask if there's something else they would like to talk about.

For example, if they need any help with the project or if there's anything they can do, like make them a snack.

The purpose of having effective communication with your teenager is to show them that no matter what's going on in your life, you will always have time for them.

Here are a few tips on how to talk with your teen:

Avoid Lecturing

If there's one thing that teenagers dislike the most, it's parent conversations starting with, "In my time…"

If your lecture starts like this, be prepared to be blocked because the more you will drone on and on about how things used to be when you were young, the more your teenager will tune you out.

Don't Act Like You Have All the Answers

If something is bothering your teenager, ask them for ideas on how to handle the situation instead of dictating what they should do.

Don't Act Judgmental

Being judgmental is the fastest way to end any form of communication with your teenager. Let's say that your teenager did something they were not supposed to. When they failed, you came at them with an "I told you so" and scolded them for their actions.

Yes, you advised them against what they were doing, and they failed, but that does not mean you judge them for it. As a parent, your most important role is to lift your child up, not bring them down!

Do Not Interrupt Your Teenager

You are in a gathering and are talking with friends and family members. Your teenager joins the circle and starts to tell a story. You suddenly interrupt in the middle and say, "This reminds me of..."

How would you feel if your teenager disrespects you in the same way? You would probably feel embarrassed. That's exactly how your teenager felt. Give respect; get respect, no matter what the age difference.

Respect Their Point of View

The world is changing at a fast pace. Parents don't know the latest trends or who's who. If your teenager has something to say, respect their point of view instead of trying to prove them wrong.

Enjoy Something Together

Having something in common with your teenager will earn you many brownie points. From a hobby to no matter what they are interested in, try to know everything about their life.

When it comes to bonding with your teenager with communication, you need to seize the moment and not wait for an opportunity to come by. Grabbing a bite to eat? Why not talk about their homework. Washing the dishes as they dry them? Ask them what's latest in their life.

Disciplining Teens

Teen years are the perfect time to practice disciplining your children. During this period, independence begins, and your teenager's rebellious phase starts.

For example, you have a 9 P.M. curfew. It means that your teenager needs to be at home after 9 P.M. All they need to tell you is where they are going and who they will be with. There are no other restrictions. They will have to check in with you occasionally, but that sounds reasonable, right?

Well, your teenager is not going to think the same. They will see this as an invasion of privacy. There are times when you have to take a step back and not interfere with what your teenager is doing, and this is not one of them.

As a parent, it is your responsibility to make sure that they are spending time in the company of a responsible teenager who knows what they are doing.

When things don't go your way, you end up disciplining your children.

So, what is it you do?

Beat them?

Shout at them?

Teach them a lesson by grounding them?

Take away their phone?

Cancel whatever plans they had made with their friends for next week?

Some of these are acceptable, and others aren't. We are sure you know which ones fall into the latter category: Physical and verbal abuse!

Completely UNACCEPTABLE!

Teenagers are full of bad decisions, and that's because they are just starting to discover life. This is why you need to strike a balance between overly permissive and overly strict, and here's how to do it:

Don't Overreact

Overreacting to anything doesn't exactly hurt your child. However, it shifts their focus from the matter at hand. Let's suppose your teenager did a good thing, but the way they did it is unacceptable. You feel it wasn't right, and so you gasp and scold them for being irresponsible.

Your reaction should have been a pat on the back with a "Well done." Until and unless they were in grave danger, you don't need to say anything. If you want to complain to someone, do it to your friend or spouse.

Set Clear Rules

The house rules should be followed by everyone and by that, we mean the parents and the children. There's no exception!

How do you trust your teenager to respect and follow you if what they do has consequences, but if you do the same thing, there are none? Just because you are the parent doesn't mean you can get away with it! Hold yourself to the same standards.

Before setting any rule, get your teenager's input on it. For example, everyone in the house has to complete their chores. Those who don't will have one hour deducted from their free time. So, if your teenager likes playing video games and you have allotted 2 hours to them, they will play only an hour the day they don't complete their chores.

As your teenager grows old, you can set more meaningful consequences if a rule is broken. For example, breaking curfew would mean they are grounded for a week, lose their cell phone, and can't invite friends.

Listen Before Reacting

You know how we parents have this knack of reacting first, creating a fuss and after listening to the full story, saying, "Well, why didn't you say that first!"

Don't worry. This happens to most parents.

Sometimes, your teenager will have a valid reason for breaking the rule. Maybe, the reason they broke curfew was that they had a flat tire or they were helping a friend in need.

Always hear what your teenager has to say first and then decide whether they should be punished or not.

The Punishment Must Fit the Crime

A broken rule should have consequences because it's the best way to teach your teenager a valuable lesson. If your teenager stays out 2 hours past the curfew, they should be punished in a way they will remember. This will stop them from making the same mistake again.

For example, you could ground them for two weeks or tell them they will be mowing their neighbor's lawn for free for two weeks.

You need to decide what consequence applies to what broken rule but remember: Check in with your teenager to make sure that they agree to the rule and its punishment. It's not about giving them a choice but making them aware that you are reasonable.

Always Follow Through

Never shrink away from your responsibility. For example, your teenager has a big game next week. They are excited about it, and in this excitement, they sneak out and go drinking with their friends. You caught them red-handed as they were climbing into their room through the window.

This is unacceptable, and so you ground them, which means they won't be taking part in the game. Your teenager will argue how you are destroying their chances of making the team, but there will be other opportunities. You talk to their football coach and come up with a solution. They will be on the team but play only if a player and the substitute player get injured.

You should always follow through because you need to show your teenager you do what you say. If you don't, they will do the same thing again, thinking they can get away with it.

Resolving Conflict

There will be plenty of times when you will find yourself holding your head and thinking, "What did I get myself into?" The subject of your misery – your teenager.

A little amount of conflict is healthy in a relationship. You know how they say, "It's a love-hate relationship?" Well, if there's no drama in your life, it becomes monotonous. The same applies to teenagers. There comes a moment when anything triggers them. That's them struggling for independence, which, in a way, is a good thing.

However, when the conflict turns into a tantrum, that's when things start to unravel. For example, your teenager wants to go to a college party, where you know there will be alcohol and possibly drugs. So, you say no. This results in a huffy attitude, followed by slamming the door and not coming for dinner.

No matter how small or big the matter, it feels like you are walking on eggshells around your teenager so that they don't get upset.

This struggle is caused by the two new directions your teenager faces. The first is showing themselves as a unique individual capable of making decisions, and the second is their desire for more freedom.

Here's a tidbit of information that will ease your mind: This conflict with you and them subsides when they turn 16.

So, what's the real reason behind the conflict? Here's an example that will help you understand this:

Suppose you have a curfew of 9 P.M. for your teenage son. Under no circumstances is he allowed to stay out late unless he stays at a friend's house. His friends start partying after 9 P.M., which upsets him, and he points this out every day.

The real conflict here is not the curfew but your reason behind it. In your eyes, you do not feel that your son is responsible enough to stay out late. He thinks you still see him as an 11-year-old who needs looking after.

If your teenager constantly argues on this matter, perhaps his maturity level is higher than you think. In this case, you need to re-evaluate your rules and involve your teenager in the next decision.

Resolving a conflict is not that big of a deal. You just need to have a strategy in mind to handle situations where you think your teenager might balk at the rules. Here's how to do it:

Pay Attention

The number one rule of resolving a conflict is paying attention to your teenager. At this stage, the conflicts are random. They are spontaneous outbursts on anything. All your teenager needs is a little amount of your time.

This might sound a bit confusing because at one point, they ask for freedom, and at others, they want your attention even though they don't ask for it. For example, your teenager is struggling at school. She shows attitude in the house and talks to you rudely. Though she wants you to know what she is going through, she doesn't know how to tell you because you might see her as weak.

You need to read between the lines and take the first step and make an effort to know what's going on in their life. You should do this at an early age so that your child comes to you with their troubles even when they grow old.

Don't Try to Resolve Matters When You Are Angry

When your teenager disagrees with you, and the conversation turns into a fight, what do you usually do?

Most parents start shouting and say, "Go to your room."

This is where the problem lies. You both are bound to end up exchanging words that will hurt each other, so the best thing to do in this situation is to walk away. You can always come back to the matter later when you have calmed down. Moreover, the time apart will give you some perspective, and you will be able to talk with your teenager without getting angry again.

Have Scheduled Conversations

If breakfast is eaten at sharp 7 in the morning and dinner is served at 8 in the night, why can't you schedule a talk with your teenager every day?

All you will do is talk about your day and ask your teenager to do the same during this time. Your teenager wants to be heard, and this is the perfect opportunity to practice empathic listening.

If you feel that the conflict might not get resolved with a talk, it's better to seek help. Resentment builds like mold, and if not addressed in time, it can grow and destroy everything. Schedule individual and family sessions with a therapist so that you can repair the bond between you and your teenager.

The Importance of Values

How does a teenager make sound decisions?

Through the personal values taught by their parents!

You might have already taught some to your child, such as respecting your elders, not lying, not talking to strangers, etc. When a child enters the teen years, these values change. Teenagers act upon these values when they are facing important life decisions. Some of the values are refined and take on a completely different view in the process.

Cultural and ethnic identity, religion, and attitude towards distant family members are some areas where values differ. Your job is to ensure that the values you taught them in infancy are still being followed in teen years.

For example, your teenager comes home after a day out with their friends and tells you all about what they did. She suddenly announces how cool it was that her friend shoplifted. You promptly set her straight, saying that stealing is a crime and that she should never do it.

When your teenager reveals something like this to you, do not be dramatic about it. You may show your disappointment but not to the degree that your teenager might stop sharing things with you.

Parents serve as role models for their children. When they are between the ages of 5 to 10, they try to imitate you. What they learn at this age is used by children to live their teenage lives.

So, before you do something that might send the wrong message to your teenager, ask yourself the following questions:

- Do you always tell the truth to your teenager?
- Do you ask your teenager to lie for you?
- Do you gossip in front of your teenager?
- Do you respect other people when you are in a social gathering?
- Do you follow healthy eating habits?
- Do you treat your life as valuable?
- Do you have hobbies that are fun for you?
- Do you have friends who come home to hang out with you?

These are the teaching moments that help you set a standard for your teenager. Through these, you can set values using your words and actions.

Respect – The Most Important Value

Respect is one of the most important values you teach in your home. In this area, you should be a role model. When children enter the teen years, they expect respect from their parents and peers.

By giving them the respect they want and deserve, you can get their attention on two fronts: You boost their self-esteem, and you mold your child into a respectable person who knows right from wrong.

Parenting styles differ from family to family. For example, one family deals with conflicts by sitting down and talking about the problem, while the other sweeps the matter under the rug and revisits it another day.

When it comes to showing respect, here are some rules you should set:

- Name-calling is not acceptable
- If you have done something wrong, accept the blame rather than putting it on someone else or giving a lame excuse.
- Bullying, either physically or verbally, will not be tolerated
- Humiliating or belittling a person to make them feel worthless is not allowed... not even as a joke between friends
- Apologize immediately and accept when you are wrong
- Do not interrupt others when they are talking
- Respect the other person's independent thoughts, property, and privacy

Never accept intolerance. For example, your teenager likes to make fun of everyone. His jokes are meant to be fun but have a mean element, which usually upsets the person the joke is directed at. When the same thing is done to him, he doesn't like it and gets angry.

One of the most important life lessons that teens must be taught is that they should never do something to others they wouldn't want done to themselves.

The good news is that you can beat intolerance with anything positive. You can share real-life examples with them on how to shed the cloak of intolerance; people can achieve success more easily.

In addition, ask your teen to share their opinion on the matter and ask questions such as, "How would you feel, if..."

You know how they say, "Respect is earned?" This is a lesson you need to teach your kids from an early age. Often, in the fight for independence and freedom, teenagers tend to neglect their responsibility. This leads to disrespect, and this behavior slowly becomes a part of everything they do and say.

So, make sure that your teenager grows up with family values and knows the importance of respecting their elders.

Teaching Your Teenager Responsibility

Encouraging your teenager to make their own decisions and then holding them accountable for the consequences makes them more independent.

In order to become a capable adult, a teenager needs to know right from wrong. There will be times when they will draw a blank, but if you do your job right, they will know how to proceed in the face of challenges.

How quickly responsibilities are handed to them depends on when you are ready. This is often a huge step for parents because they feel as if they are severing one of the ties that held them and their children close.

The No, Yes, and Maybe Options

Not all parents are able to give teenagers responsibility. It's not because they don't believe in them but because they aren't ready to let go yet.

Here's how you can decide:

The Yes Option

If you feel that your child might be dealing with some issues, then you can choose 'yes' for the following reasons:

- They are ready to ride or walk to school alone
- They might be open to cooking a meal for the family, at least once a week
- They might be open to paying for something they want and have been saving for it for a while

- They don't need your help with making a small decision such as what clothes to wear, which hairstyle looks the best, etc.

In the 'yes' option, you agree that whatever your teen's decision might be, you will accept it. When your teenager handles the responsibility well, show your approval by praising them. However, if you feel that your teenager has made the wrong decision, then stand back and observe. Do not interfere unless your child is in danger.

The No Option

Always assess the situation first before giving your teenager responsibility. If you feel that they might get injured in the midst, then say a resounding NO.

For example, your teenager wants to try alcohol. Not only are they not of legal drinking age, but the negative effects of it on such a young mind can destroy their future. Another example is that they want to buy something that costs a lot.

Managing the 'no' can be difficult at times because it relies on setting clear limits and good communication. Rather than forbidding your teenager from a task, explain to them why their decision is not a good idea. Remember: The key to making sure they listen to you is your calm demeanor. If you lose control, they will use it to emotionally manipulate you.

The Maybe Option

The 'maybe' option is referred to as the gray area. There's always room to turn a 'no' into 'yes,' but as the parent, you have to decide which decision gets the vote.

For example, you might be open to allowing your teenager to try something new that is low on the danger scale. Negotiating a 'no' shows your teenager that you are open to possibilities if they can argue reasonably.

Tips on How to Make Your Teenager More Responsible

The only reason your teenager might balk at taking responsibility is that they are too lazy. However, you will find them arguing with you during a fight that they are all grown up now and can do their own things.

Responsibility requires motivation. Your teenager might be open to driving a car because he is 15 now, but when you ask them to do the chores, they suddenly have homework to do.

Following are some tips on how to raise a responsible teenager:

Stop Doing Their Chores

What do you do when your teenager refuses to do something that you asked for? Do you listen to them nag and wail for hours before you give in and do the chore yourself, or do you force them to do something and, if they don't, threaten them with taking away one of their privileges?

That's not how you handle insubordination. The plain and simple way to go about this is to stop doing their chores altogether. For example, how hard can it be to do a load of laundry? All you have to do is separate the whites from the colorful ones, measure the washing liquid, fill the machine with water and rotate the dial. If your teenager can't do this, then stop doing it for them. They won't survive for long once they run out of clean underpants.

Tell Them to Volunteer

The reward of volunteering is great. It will make your teenager understand that sometimes, everything is not about them. There are other people and things in the world that need attention.

When your teenager is involved in any cause that brings joy to people, they will realize how difficult life can be and how privileged they are. Some parents think they need to knock them off their feet to teach them a lesson. We say that you can do the same thing by making them commit to a meaningful task.

For example, your teenager could volunteer at a food shelter during Christmas. This will show them how there are many starving people in the world, and the amount of food coming in will teach them about the importance of food.

They could volunteer at a local hospital that has a children's cancer ward. By interacting with these sick children, they will learn the importance of patience and how they need to be happy with even the smallest of achievements.

Every good act they do will show them how a positive gesture on their part can bring a smile on their loved ones' faces or that of strangers... and, most importantly, make them feel good about themselves.

Recognize Their Responsibility Cues

As mentioned earlier, every teenager is different. For example, some teenagers have a knack for absorbing things around them. This not only makes them smart, but they can also complete tasks exceptionally fast.

Let's say that your teenager has gotten really good at making a snack for themselves and their siblings. You know that there won't be any disasters if they are alone in the kitchen and the house.

So, you decide to test their level of handling responsibilities by leaving them in charge while you complete a couple of outside chores.

Model Responsibility

Have you ever been in an argument with your teenager regarding how irresponsible you are, and you have the nerve to teach them? While they might be acting out of line, they are not wrong if you shirk your responsibilities from time to time in front of them.

In order to make them more responsible, you need to model the act so that they can see for themselves how you handle things. Do not play the "I am the parent, and so this doesn't apply to me" card.

Teach Them Time Management

One responsibility that all teenagers need to have is time management. It teaches them good behavior and turns them into reliable people, who people can trust. However, it can be a tad bit difficult to teach them this skill because teenagers don't exactly go about their day looking at the clock.

You can't reason with teenagers about this because they are more interested in hanging out with their friends or playing video games after finishing their homework.

So, what could push you and them to put in a little extra effort? Well, here's something that will help you change their mind: Teenagers who know how to budget their time can make better decisions. Like many other lessons, this too is one that should be taught by parents.

Let's say that you are disorganized or frequently late. The first thing you do is make excuses about your tardiness. Expect your teenager to do the same because they are more likely to follow in your footsteps in an attempt to imitate you.

Here's an example to help you understand this:

Teenagers have a lot of commitments, which include school and extracurricular activities, not to mention their leisure time.

One constant is their homework, which they have to complete no matter what. This is where organizational skills come in. Carve out some time from your schedule to teach them the importance of scheduling and planning.

Doing this together allows you and your teenager to handle this as a team. Moreover, with a routine in place, you can find out how your teenager is handling the responsibilities. It might be rough on them sometimes when they are juggling college, personal and family life, so support them when they need you.

Raising a responsible teenager is all about teaching them accountability. In conclusion, when you stop doing their chores, you teach them independence. When you recognize that they are ready to take on more, you make them feel like an older person who can be independent. Modeling responsibility for them sets a standard and shows them that you have set rules for yourself too. Lastly, time management allows them to do things they like, while also handling their responsibilities.

Conclusion

Teenagers want a friend and not a parent. Period.

They want someone to listen to them, not judge them, and at the same time, provide them with valuable advice. However, they can't have the best of both worlds. This is why you need to manage the parent and friend role side by side.

Your teenager's personality also plays an important role in how you parent them. As mentioned earlier, there are multiple types of teenagers, but most are divided into standard categories. Their moods can range from being angry at the smallest things to being a drama queen, while their attitude can manifest in the form of carelessly shrugging responsibilities to risk-taking, making them difficult to pin down as they come with a unique set of pros and cons.

If you find yourself in a corner, always take the path of communication to reach them. The teenager dilemma will always confuse you but punishing your teenager is not the answer. You always need to reason with them so that they can understand where you are coming from.

When it comes to disciplining your child, NEVER ever raise your hand because it will accomplish nothing. You need to teach them valuable things by promoting their self-esteem, paying close attention to what they are doing, respecting their privacy, attending school events, supporting them instead of criticizing them, respecting their concerns, and not teasing them.

Don't overreact when disciplining your teenager because it will make them think twice before opening up to you again. Don't forget to set clear rules and always ask for their input to make sure that they are on board with the consequences.

We can't stress enough how important it is to communicate effectively with your teenager. There are certain things that you shouldn't do, such as lecturing, acting like you have all the answers, being judgmental, interrupting them, not respecting their point of view and not having time for them.

These are what cause conflicts, which can only be resolved by paying attention, resolving matters when you have calmed down and scheduling conversations so that you can stay up to date on what is happening in your teenager's life.

This will teach your teenager how to respect you and handle responsibilities that are given to them rather than fall on them.

In conclusion, the best way to raise a teenager is to talk with them, listen to them and give them only so much they can handle without thinking they will fail.

Disclaimer

Copyright © Year 2022 – All Rights Reserved.

No part of this eBook can be transmitted or reproduced in any form, including print, electronic, photocopying, scanning, mechanical, or recording, without prior written permission from the author.

This eBook has been written for information purposes only. Every effort has been made to make this eBook as complete and accurate as possible. However, there may be mistakes in typography or content.

The purpose of this eBook is to encourage people to invest in their lives and do things during their life that they can rejoice in going back to their old age. The author and the publisher do not warrant that the information contained in this eBook is fully complete and shall not be responsible for any errors or omissions. The author and publisher shall have neither liability nor responsibility to any person or entity concerning any loss or damage caused or alleged to be caused directly or indirectly by this eBook.